Scott Foresman - Addison Wesley

MATH

Review From Last Year Masters

Grade 3

Scott Foresman - Addison Wesley

Editorial Offices: Glenview, Illinois • New York, New York
Sales Offices: Reading, Massachusetts • Duluth, Georgia • Glenview, Illinois
Carrollton, Texas • Menlo Park, California

http://www.sf.aw.com

Overview

Review From Last Year Masters provides a review of key concepts from the previous year of Scott Foresman - Addison Wesley MATH. Each of the 20 masters begins with an instructional model that is followed by practice.

Review From Last Year Masters can be used to determine how well students have retained concepts from the previous year and to prepare students for the upcoming year.

The *Answers and Options for Further Review* section at the back of this book provides alternatives for students who need additional reteaching and practice. Materials from the previous year (Student Edition lessons, Reteaching Masters, and Practice Masters) are keyed to each master.

ISBN 0-201-48882-5

Copyright © Addison Wesley Longman, Inc.

Printed in the United States of America

3 4 5 6 7 8 9 10 – CRK – 03 02 01 00

Contents

Number Patterns

Continue the pattern.

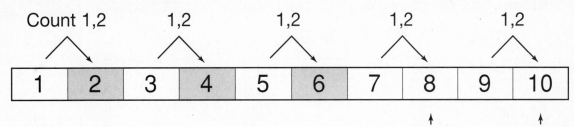

Count 1,2   1,2   1,2   1,2   1,2

1	2	3	4	5	6	7	8	9	10

Next is **8,** then **10.**

Continue the patterns. Color the numbers.

1.

1	2	3	4	5	6	7	8	9	10
11	12	13	14	15	16	17	18	19	20
21	22	23	24	25	26	27	28	29	30
31	32	33	34	35	36	37	38	39	40

2.

1	2	3	4	5	6	7	8	9	10
11	12	13	14	15	16	17	18	19	20
21	22	23	24	25	26	27	28	29	30
31	32	33	34	35	36	37	38	39	40

3.

1	2	3	4	5	6	7	8	9	10
11	12	13	14	15	16	17	18	19	20
21	22	23	24	25	26	27	28	29	30
31	32	33	34	35	36	37	38	39	40

Problem Solving: Graphing

Each **table** or **graph** shows data on how students get to school.

Tally

How	Tally	Total
Bike	I	1
Bus	IIII I	6
Car	III	3
Walk	IIII	4

Pictograph

Bike	🧍
Bus	🧍🧍🧍🧍🧍🧍
Car	🧍🧍🧍
Walk	🧍🧍🧍🧍

Each 🧍 means 1 child

Bar Graph

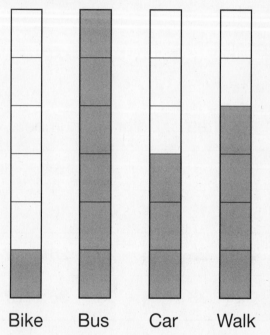

Bike   Bus   Car   Walk

Use the tally data to complete each table or graph.

My Favorite Season

Tally

Season	Tally	Total
Summer	IIII I	
Fall	II	2
Winter	IIII	
Spring	III	

Pictograph

Summer	
Fall	
Winter	
Spring	

Each ☺ means 1 child

Bar Graph

Summer   Fall   Winter   Spring

Explore Addition and Subtraction

Brad's team had 4 .

They bought 5 more .

How many did they have?

Use counters.

4 + 5 = 9

A pond had 8 .

3  went away.

How many were left?

Use counters.

①②③④⑤⑥⑦⑧

8 − 3 = 5

Solve each problem. Use counters.

1. 7 were turned on.

Meg turned 5 off.

How many were left on?

7 − 5 = _____

2. 2 were in the

lost and found.

4 more were found.

How many in all?

2 + 4 = _____

3. A carpenter had 6 .

He lost 2 .

How many were left?

6 − 2 = _____

4. Jan used 3 to paint her

room. She used 6 more to

paint the garage. How many

did she use in all?

3 + 6 = _____

5. There were 9 on a tree.

4 fell off.

How many were left? _____

Name _____

Addition to 18

Find 6 + 7.

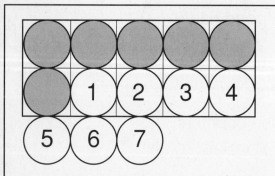

6 counters are on the ten frame.

4 of 7 counters make a 10.

3 left over make 13.

6 + 7 = 13

Find each sum.

1.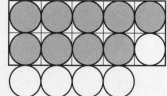

9 + 5 = _____

2.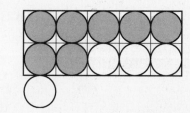

7 + 4 = _____

3. 8 + 6 = _____   7 + 8 = _____   9 + 6 = _____

4. 6 + 10 = _____   9 + 8 = _____   8 + 8 = _____

5. 7 + 5 = _____   8 + 9 = _____   9 + 9 = _____

6. 10 + 7 = _____   7 + 7 = _____   8 + 4 = _____

7. Mark made 5 phone calls during the
week. He made 10 calls on the weekend.
How many calls did he make in all?   _____

Name _____

Subtraction to 18

Find 14 − 7.

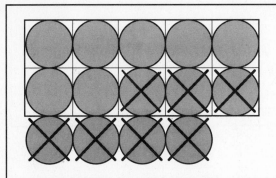

14 counters are shaded.

7 are crossed out.

7 counters are left.

14 − 7 = 7

Find each difference.

1.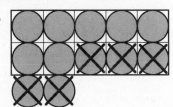

12 − 5 = _____

2.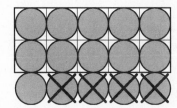

15 − 4 = _____

Subtract.

3. 18 − 9 = _____   14 − 9 = _____   7 − 5 = _____

4. 11 − 9 = _____   9 − 6 = _____   17 − 6 = _____

5. 13 − 6 = _____   11 − 4 = _____   8 − 3 = _____

6. 12 − 8 = _____   16 − 5 = _____   16 − 9 = _____

7. Tania saved $15. She spent $8 on a gift for
her brother. How much did she have left?

_____

Fact Families

Complete the fact family. Add or subtract.

All the facts in a fact family use the same numbers. This fact family uses 6, 9, and 15.

$6 + 9 = 15$ $15 - 9 = 6$

$9 + 6 = 15$ $15 - 6 = 9$

Complete each fact family. Add or subtract.

1.

$8 + 5 =$ _____

$5 + 8 =$ _____

$13 - 5 =$ _____

$13 - 8 =$ _____

2.

$8 + 9 =$ _____

$9 + 8 =$ _____

$17 - 9 =$ _____

$17 - 8 =$ _____

3.

$6 + 4 =$ _____

$4 + 6 =$ _____

$10 - 4 =$ _____

$10 - 6 =$ _____

4.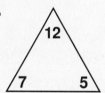

$7 + 5 =$ _____

$5 + 7 =$ _____

$12 - 5 =$ _____

$12 - 7 =$ _____

5.

$8 + 6 =$ _____

$6 + 8 =$ _____

$14 - 6 =$ _____

$14 - 8 =$ _____

6.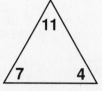

$7 + 4 =$ _____

$4 + 7 =$ _____

$11 - 4 =$ _____

$11 - 7 =$ _____

7. One fact in a fact family is $16 - 7 = 9$.

What are the other facts?

_____

_____

_____

Numbers to 100

The number 75 comes after 74 and before 76.

| 70 | 71 | 72 | 73 | 74 | 75 | 76 | 77 | 78 | 79 |

Write the missing numbers.

1	2	3						9	
				15			18		20
21					26				
			34			37			
	42								50
		53			56				
			64			67			
	72							79	
81									90
				95			98		

Write the missing numbers.

1. 80, 81, 82, _____, _____, _____, _____, _____, _____ .

2. _____, _____, 95, 96, _____, _____, _____, _____

Name _____

Money

Count on to find how much money.

25,　　35, 45, 55,　　60,　　61, 62, 63, 64　　| 64¢ |

Start.　　Count by 10s,　　by 5s,　　and by 1s.

Count on to find how much. Write the total.

1.

　　25,　35, ____, ____, ____, ____, ____, ____　　| | ¢

2.

____, ____, ____, ____, ____, ____, ____, ____　　| | ¢

3.

____, ____, ____, ____, ____, ____, ____, ____　　| | ¢

4. Draw 6 coins to make 38¢.

Time

Write the time.

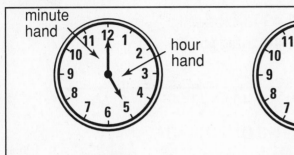  

5:00   5:15   5:30

Write the time.

1.

_____:_____

2.

_____:_____

3.

_____:_____

4.

_____:_____

5.

_____:_____

6.

_____:_____

7.

_____:_____

8.

_____:_____

9.

_____:_____

Estimating Sums and Differences

Estimate the sum of 26 + 43. Use nearest tens.

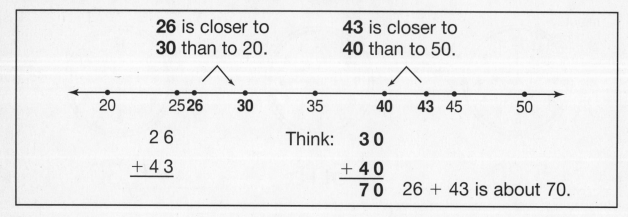

26 is closer to **30** than to 20.

43 is closer to **40** than to 50.

```
 2 6
+4 3
```

Think:
```
  3 0
+ 4 0
  7 0
```
26 + 43 is about 70.

Estimate the sum or difference. Use nearest tens.

1.
```
   1 9   Think:  2 0
 + 7 2        +  7 0
```

19 + 72 is about _____.

2.
```
   5 7   Think:  ⬜
 − 3 8        −  ⬜
```

57 − 38 is about _____.

3.
```
   8 2   Think:  ⬜
 − 2 9        −  ⬜
```

82 − 29 is about _____.

4.
```
   3 7   Think:  ⬜
 + 4 7        +  ⬜
```

37 + 47 is about _____.

5.
```
   4 6   Think:  ⬜
 + 4 3        +  ⬜
```

46 + 43 is about _____.

6.
```
   7 4   Think:  ⬜
 − 5 1        −  ⬜
```

74 − 51 is about _____.

7. Marcus has 51 Space Race toys. Reynaldo has 28 Space Race toys. About how many more does Marcus have than Reynaldo has? _____

Two-Digit Addition

Find 24 + 63.   Find 37 + 59.

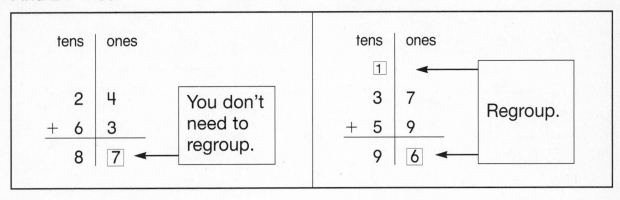

tens	ones
2	4
+ 6	3
8	[7]

You don't need to regroup.

tens	ones
[1]	
3	7
+ 5	9
9	[6]

Regroup.

Add. Regroup if needed.

1.
tens	ones
[1]	
2	4
+ 4	9
	3

2.
tens	ones
[ ]	
2	7
+ 6	2

3.
tens	ones
[ ]	
4	5
+ 3	5

4.
tens	ones
[ ]	
1	0
+ 8	4

5.
tens	ones
[ ]	
6	6
+ 2	1

6.
tens	ones
[ ]	
3	7
+ 5	8

7.
tens	ones
[ ]	
2	9
+ 6	1

8.
tens	ones
[ ]	
4	4
+ 4	5

9.
tens	ones
[ ]	
8	1
+	9

10. Tom had three suitcases weighing 35 lb, 27 lb, and 23 lb. How much did they weigh altogether?

Two-Digit Subtraction

Find 87 − 24.   Find 42 − 15.

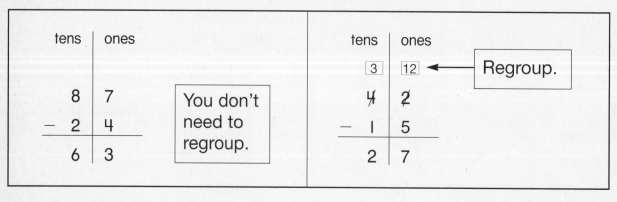

tens	ones
8	7
− 2	4
6	3

You don't need to regroup.

tens	ones
3	12
4̷	2̷
− 1	5
2	7

Regroup.

Subtract. Regroup if needed.

1.
tens	ones
4	11
5̷	1̷
− 2	3
	8

2.
tens	ones
7	8
− 2	4

3.
tens	ones
3	7
− 1	5

4.
tens	ones
6	4
− 2	9

5.
tens	ones
8	2
− 3	5

6.
tens	ones
4	0
− 2	7

7.
tens	ones
9	3
− 4	3

8.
tens	ones
2	8
− 1	9

9.
tens	ones
5	7
− 4	2

10. Mary had 44 books. She sold 27 of them at a garage sale. How many did she have left?

_____

Numbers to 1,000

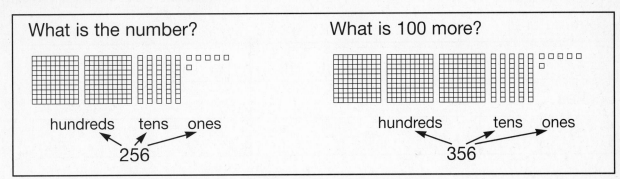

What is the number?

hundreds   tens   ones

256

What is 100 more?

hundreds   tens   ones

356

Write the number. Draw blocks to show the number more or less.

1. What is the number?

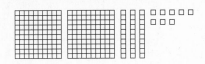

_____ _____ _____

What is 100 more?

_____ _____ _____

2. What is the number?

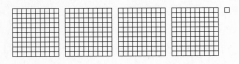

_____ _____ _____

What is 100 less?

_____ _____ _____

3. What is the number?

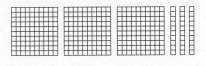

_____ _____ _____

What is 300 more?

_____ _____ _____

4. What is the number?

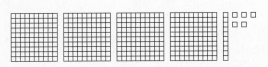

_____ _____ _____

What is 300 less?

_____ _____ _____

Length

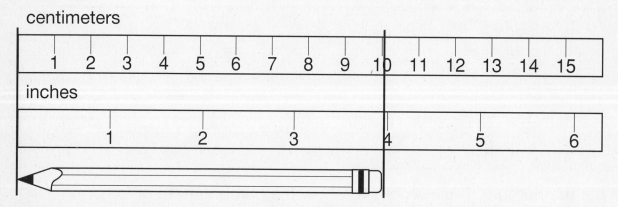

This pencil is about 10 centimeters. It is about 4 inches long.

Estimate. Then measure using inches.

1.

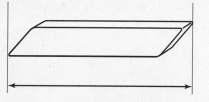

Estimate. _____ inches

Measure. _____ inches

2.

BLUE

Estimate. _____ inches

Measure. _____ inches

Estimate. Then measure using centimeters.

3.

Estimate. _____ centimeters

Measure. _____ centimeters

4.

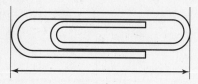

Estimate. _____ centimeters

Measure. _____ centimeters

5. Start at the dot. Draw a line about 5 inches long.

•

6. Start at the dot. Draw a line about 11 centimeters long.

•

Solids

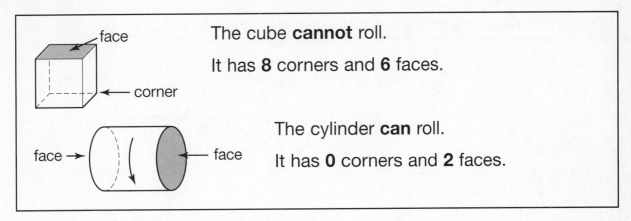

The cube **cannot** roll.

It has **8** corners and **6** faces.

The cylinder **can** roll.

It has **0** corners and **2** faces.

Complete the table.

Solid	Roll?	Shape of Face	Number of Corners	Number of Faces
1.	No			
2.				
3.				
4.				
5.				

Shapes

Faces of solids are shapes. Some shapes have names.

Rectangle   Square   Triangle   Circle

Draw the shape on the **bottom** of the solid. Name the shape.

1.

shape _____

2.

Juice

shape _____

3.

shape _____

4.

shape _____

5.

Milk

shape _____

Fractions

Write the fraction for parts that are shaded.

 **3** parts shaded
4 parts in all
$\frac{3}{4}$ is shaded.

 2 parts shaded
5 parts in all
$\frac{2}{5}$ is shaded.

Write the fraction for parts that are shaded.

1.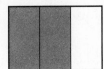

_____ parts shaded.

_____ parts in all.

_____ is shaded.

2.

_____

3.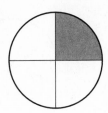

_____

4.

_____

5.

_____

6.

_____

Shade each fraction.

7. Shade $\frac{3}{4}$.

8. Shade $\frac{1}{3}$.

9. Shade $\frac{4}{6}$.

10. Shade $\frac{5}{8}$.

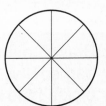

Name _____

Probability

Would you more likely spin stars or spin stripes?

more likely stars

more likely stripes

Circle the more likely spin.

1. 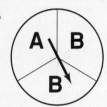   more likely A
more likely B

2. 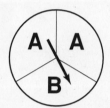   more likely A
more likely B

3. 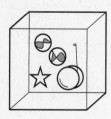   more likely 1
more likely 2
more likely 3

4. 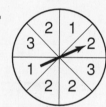   more likely 1
more likely 2
more likely 3

Circle whether you will always, sometimes, or never pick an object.

5. Pick a marble.

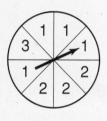   always
sometimes
never

6. Pick a star.

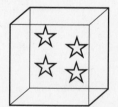   always
sometimes
never

7. Draw 5 marbles in your bag so you could never pick a blue marble.

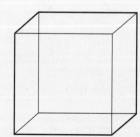

Multiplication Concepts

Show 3 × 2. Show 2 × 3.

You can add or multiply to find how many in all.	You can multiply numbers in any order and get the same product.
○ ○ ○ ○ ○ ○ 2 + 2 + 2 = 6 3 × 2 = 6	○ ○ ○ ○ ○ ○ ○ ○ ○ ○ 　　　　　○ ○ 3 × 2 = 6　　2 × 3 = 6

Draw groups. Find the product.

1. Draw groups to show 4 × 2.

○ ○ ○ ○
○ ○ ○ ○

How many in all? _____

2. Draw groups to show 2 × 4.

How many in all? _____

3. Draw groups to show 4 × 3.

How many in all? _____

4. Draw groups to show 5 × 1.

How many in all? _____

5. Draw groups to show 5 × 3.

How many in all? _____

6. Draw groups to show 2 × 2.

How many in all? _____

7. Does 5 rows of 2 counters have more counters than 2 rows of 5 counters? Explain.

_____

Division Concepts

Show 6 ÷ 3.   Show 6 ÷ 2.

Divide 6 counters into 3 equal groups to find the answer.	*Divide 6 counters into 2 equal groups to find the answer.*
There are 2 counters in each group. So, 6 ÷ 3 = 2.	There are 3 counters in each group. So, 6 ÷ 2 = 3.

Draw groups. Complete the number sentence.

1. Draw groups to show 4 ÷ 2.

     4 ÷ 2 = _____

2. Draw groups to show 8 ÷ 2.

     8 ÷ 2 = _____

3. Draw groups to show 5 ÷ 1.

     5 ÷ 1 = _____

4. Draw groups to show 10 ÷ 5.

     10 ÷ 5 = _____

5. Draw groups to show 7 ÷ 7.

     7 ÷ 7 = _____

6. Draw groups to show 20 ÷ 4.

     20 ÷ 4 = _____

7. Tanisha has 15 books. She gives 5 books to each friend. How many friends get books from Tanisha?

_____

© Scott Foresman Addison Wesley 3

Answers and Options for Further Review

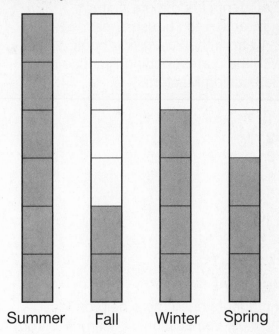

Summer   Fall   Winter   Spring

REVIEW 1

If students need more help on number patterns, use Lesson 1-4 from the 2nd-grade book, along with the corresponding Practice and Reteaching Masters.

1. 20, 25, 30, 35, 40
2. 12, 15, 18, 21, 24, 27, 30, 33, 36, 39
3. 24, 30, 36

REVIEW 2

If students need more help on graphing, use Lessons 1-5 through 1-8 from the 2nd-grade book, along with the corresponding Practice and Reteaching Masters.

My Favorite Season
Tally

Season	Tally	Total
Summer	JHH I	6
Fall	II	2
Winter	IIII	4
Spring	III	3

Pictograph

Summer	☺☺☺☺☺☺
Fall	☺☺
Winter	☺☺☺☺
Spring	☺☺☺

Each ☺ means 1 child

REVIEW 3

If students need more help on exploring addition and subtraction, use Lessons 2-1 and 2-7 from the 2nd-grade book, along with the corresponding Practice and Reteaching Masters.

1. 2 lights   **2.** 6 hats
3. 4 hammers   **4.** 9 paint cans
5. 5 leaves

REVIEW 4

If students need more help on addition to 18, use Lessons 2-2 and 2-3 from the 2nd-grade book, along with the corresponding Practice and Reteaching Masters.

1. 14   **2.** 11
3. 14   15   15
4. 16   17   16
5. 12   17   18
6. 17   14   12
7. 15 calls

REVIEW 5

If students need more help on subtraction to 18, use Lessons 2-7 to 2-10 from the 2nd-grade book, along with the corresponding Practice and Reteaching Masters.

1. 7		
2. 11		
3. 9	5	2
4. 2	3	11
5. 7	7	5
6. 4	11	7
7. $7		

REVIEW 6

If students need more help on fact families, use Lessons 4-1 and 4-2 from the 2nd-grade book, along with the corresponding Practice and Reteaching Masters.

1. 13, 13, 8, 5
2. 17, 17, 8, 9
3. 10, 10, 6, 4
4. 12, 12, 7, 5
5. 14, 14, 8, 6
6. 11, 11, 7, 4
7. $16 - 9 = 7, 7 + 9 = 16, 9 + 7 = 16$

REVIEW 7

If students need more help on numbers to 100, use Lessons 5-3 through 5-6 from the 2nd-grade book, along with the corresponding Practice and Reteaching Masters.

1	2	3	4	5	6	7	8	9	10
11	12	13	14	15	16	17	18	19	20
21	22	23	24	25	26	27	28	29	30
31	32	33	34	35	36	37	38	39	40
41	42	43	44	45	46	47	48	49	50
51	52	53	54	55	56	57	58	59	60
61	62	63	64	65	66	67	68	69	70
71	72	73	74	75	76	77	78	79	80
81	82	83	84	85	86	87	88	89	90
91	92	93	94	95	96	97	98	99	100

1. 83, 84, 85, 86, 87, 88
2. 93, 94, 97, 98, 99, 100

REVIEW 8

If students need more help on money, use Lessons 6-1 and 6-2 from the 2nd-grade book, along with the corresponding Practice and Reteaching Masters.

1. 40, 45, 50, 55, 56, 57; 57¢
2. 25, 35, 45, 55, 65, 66, 67, 68; 68¢
3. 25, 50, 60, 70, 75, 80, 85, 86; 86¢
4. Q, N, N, P, P, P

REVIEW 9

If students need more help on time, use Lessons 7-3, 7-7, and 7-8 from the 2nd-grade book, along with the corresponding Practice and Reteaching Masters.

1. 2:00	**2.** 4:15	**3.** 6:30
4. 1:30	**5.** 11:00	**6.** 7:00
7. 2:15	**8.** 10:30	**9.** 6:15

REVIEW 10

If students need more help on estimating sums and differences, use Lessons 8-4 and 9-3 from the 2nd-grade book, along with the corresponding Practice and Reteaching Masters.

1. 90   **2.** 20   **3.** 50   **4.** 90
5. 90   **6.** 20   **7.** 20 more toys

REVIEW 11

If students need more help on 2-digit addition, use Lessons 8-9 and 8-10 from the 2nd-grade book, along with the corresponding Practice and Reteaching Masters.

1. 73   **2.** 89   **3.** 80
4. 94   **5.** 87   **6.** 95
7. 90   **8.** 89   **9.** 90
10. 85 lb

REVIEW 12

If students need more help on 2-digit subtraction, use Lessons 9-8 through 9-10 from the 2nd-grade book, along with the corresponding Practice and Reteaching Masters.

1. 28   **2.** 54   **3.** 22
4. 35   **5.** 47   **6.** 13
7. 50   **8.** 9   **9.** 15
10. 17 books

REVIEW 13

If students need more help on numbers to 1,000, use Lessons 10-1 through 10-5 from the 2nd-grade book, along with the corresponding Practice and Reteaching Masters.

1. 238, ▦▦▦▦▥, 338

2. 401, ▦▦▦, 301

3. 330, ▦▦▦▦▦▦▥, 630

4. 415, ▦▥, 115

REVIEW 14

If students need more help on length, use Lessons 11-2 through 11-4 from the 2nd-grade book, along with the corresponding Practice and Reteaching Masters.

Estimates may vary.
1. 2 inches   **2.** 3 inches
3. 7 centimeters   **4.** 5 centimeters
5–6. Check students' drawings.

REVIEW 15

If students need more help on solids, use Lessons 12-1 and 12-2 from the 2nd-grade book, along with the corresponding Practice and Reteaching Masters.

Solid	Roll?	Shape of Face	Number of Corners	Number of Faces
1.	No		4	4
2.	Yes		0	2
3.	No		8	6
4.	Yes	None	0	0
5.	Yes		6	5

REVIEW 16

If students need more help on shapes, use Lesson 12-3 from the 2nd-grade book, along with the corresponding Practice and Reteaching Masters.

1. square

2. circle

3. triangle

4. rectangle

5. square

REVIEW 17

If students need more help on fractions, use Lessons 12-9 through 12-13 from the 2nd-grade book, along with the corresponding Practice and Reteaching Masters.

1. $\frac{2}{3}$ **2.** $\frac{1}{4}$ **3.** $\frac{1}{2}$

4. $\frac{4}{5}$ **5.** $\frac{6}{9}$ **6.** $\frac{2}{4}$

7.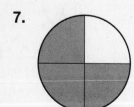

8.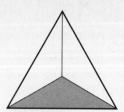

9.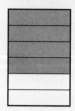

10.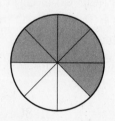

REVIEW 18

If students need more help on probability, use Lesson 12-14 from the 2nd-grade book, along with the corresponding Practice and Reteaching Masters.

1. B   **2.** A   **3.** 1   **4.** 2
5. sometimes   **6.** always
7. Drawings will vary. Students should show 5 marbles, none of which is blue.

REVIEW 19

If students need more help on multiplication concepts, use Lessons 13-1 through 13-5 from the 2nd-grade book, along with the corresponding Practice and Reteaching Masters.

1. 8 in all

2. 0 0   8 in all
   0 0
   0 0
   0 0

3. 0 0 0 0   12 in all
   0 0 0 0
   0 0 0 0

4. 0 0 0 0 0   5 in all

5. 0 0 0 0 0   15 in all
   0 0 0 0 0
   0 0 0 0 0

6. 0 0   4 in all
   0 0

7. No. You can multiply numbers in any order and get the same product.

REVIEW 20

If students need more help on division concepts, use Lessons 13-7 and 13-8 from the 2nd-grade book, along with the corresponding Practice and Reteaching Masters.

1. 2

2.

| O O O O |
| O O O O |

4

3.

| O O O O O |

5

4.

| O O |
| O O |
| O O |
| O O |
| O O |

2

5.

| O | O | O | O | O | O | O |

1

6.

| O O O O O |
| O O O O O |
| O O O O O |
| O O O O O |

5

7. 3 friends